ADVANCED SET #2

RUDIMENTS EXAM SERIES

By Glory St. Germain ARCT RMT MYCC UMTC &
Shelagh McKibbon-U'Ren RMT UMTC

ULTIMATE
MUSIC THEORY

GSG MUSIC

Enriching Lives Through Music Education

ISBN: 978-1-927641-07-1

The Ultimate Music Theory™ Program
Enriching Lives Through Music Education

The Ultimate Music Theory™ Workbooks & Answer Books Program includes:

UMT Rudiments Workbooks for Prep 1, Prep 2, Basic, Intermediate, Advanced & Complete
UMT Exam Series (Set #1 & Set #2) for Preparatory, Basic, Intermediate & Advanced

Supplemental Workbooks for PREP LEVEL, LEVELS 1 - 8 & COMPLETE LEVEL
UMT Supplemental Exam Series for LEVEL 5, LEVEL 6, LEVEL 7 & LEVEL 8

The Ultimate Music Theory Program is the *Way to Score Success* as UMT helps students prepare for nationally recognized theory examinations including the Royal Conservatory of Music.

 Library and Archives Canada Cataloguing in Publication. UMT Workbooks & Exam Series /Glory St. Germain & Shelagh McKibbon-U'Ren. Respect Copyright. All rights reserved. GlorylandPublishing.com

Ultimate Music Theory Rudiments Exam Series

GP - EPS1	ISBN: 978-1-927641-00-2	Preparatory Rudiments Exams Set #1
GP - EPS1A	ISBN: 978-1-927641-08-8	Preparatory Exams Answers Set #1
GP - EPS2	ISBN: 978-1-927641-01-9	Preparatory Rudiments Exams Set #2
GP - EPS2A	ISBN: 978-1-927641-09-5	Preparatory Exams Answers Set #2
GP - EBS1	ISBN: 978-1-927641-02-6	Basic Rudiments Exams Set #1
GP - EBS1A	ISBN: 978-1-927641-10-1	Basic Exams Answers Set #1
GP - EBS2	ISBN: 978-1-927641-03-3	Basic Rudiments Exams Set #2
GP - EBS2A	ISBN: 978-1-927641-11-8	Basic Exams Answers Set #2
GP - EIS1	ISBN: 978-1-927641-04-0	Intermediate Rudiments Exams Set #1
GP - EIS1A	ISBN: 978-1-927641-12-5	Intermediate Exams Answers Set #1
GP - EIS2	ISBN: 978-1-927641-05-7	Intermediate Rudiments Exams Set #2
GP - EIS2A	ISBN: 978-1-927641-13-2	Intermediate Exams Answers Set #2
GP - EAS1	ISBN: 978-1-927641-06-4	Advanced Rudiments Exams Set #1
GP - EAS1A	ISBN: 978-1-927641-14-9	Advanced Exams Answers Set #1
GP - EAS2	ISBN: 978-1-927641-07-1	Advanced Rudiments Exams Set #2
GP - EAS2A	ISBN: 978-1-927641-15-6	Advanced Exams Answers Set #2

Ultimate Music Theory Supplemental Exam Series

GP-L5E	ISBN: 978-1-990358-11-1	LEVEL 5 Exams
GP-L5EA	ISBN: 978-1-990358-12-8	LEVEL 5 Exams Answers
GP-L6E	ISBN: 978-1-990358-13-5	LEVEL 6 Exams
GP-L6EA	ISBN: 978-1-990358-14-2	LEVEL 6 Exams Answers
GP-L7E	ISBN: 978-1-990358-15-9	LEVEL 7 Exams
GP-L7EA	ISBN: 978-1-990358-16-6	LEVEL 7 Exams Answers
GP-L8E	ISBN: 978-1-990358-17-3	LEVEL 8 Exams
GP-L8EA	ISBN: 978-1-990358-18-0	LEVEL 8 Exams Answers

Go to UltimateMusicTheory.com and check out the FREE Resources

Ultimate Music Theory FREE RESOURCES created just for you!

The **Ultimate Music Theory Exams** reinforce the **UMT Advanced Rudiments Workbook**.

Advanced Rudiments Theory Examination requirements include Intermediate Rudiments requirements plus the following:

Clefs
- Alto Clef and Tenor Clef (C Clefs)

Rhythm - Simple, Compound and Hybrid
- Time Signatures for hybrid meters (Example: $\frac{5}{4}$, $\frac{7}{8}$ and $\frac{10}{16}$)

Scales in Major and minor keys up to and including seven sharps and seven flats
- Write or identify: Major and minor (natural, harmonic and melodic) scales, ascending and descending, beginning on any scale degree
- Write or identify: Modes (Dorian, Phrygian, Lydian, Mixolydian and Aeolian), beginning on any note

Chords
- Write or identify: all triads (Major, minor, Augmented and diminished) in root position and inversions (close position or open position)
- Write or identify: Dominant 7th chords in Major and minor keys in root position and inversions (close position or open position)
- Write or identify: diminished 7th chords of harmonic minor scales, root position only
- Identify: the scale (Major, natural minor or harmonic minor) in which a group of triads or chords may be found

Intervals - Perfect, Major and minor
- Write or identify: above or below a given note, all intervals and their inversions, melodic or harmonic form (with or without a Key Signature), including simple intervals, compound intervals and enharmonic equivalents

Transposition (Major and minor keys up to and including seven sharps and seven flats)
- Transpose a melody up or down any interval within the octave
- Rewrite a melody at the same pitch in an alternate clef (including C Clefs)
- Transpose to concert pitch a single line of music for the following orchestral instruments: Clarinet in B flat, Trumpet in B flat, French Horn in F or English Horn in F

Cadences in all Major and harmonic minor keys
- Identify the following cadences:
    Perfect (Authentic): V - I or V^7- I (Major) and V - i or V^7 - i (minor); Plagal: IV - I (Major) and iv - i (minor); Imperfect (Half Cadence): I - V or IV - V (Major) and i - V or iv - V (minor)
- Write the following cadences in keyboard style at the end of a melodic fragment:
    Perfect (Authentic): V - I (Major) and V - i (minor); Plagal: IV - I (Major) and iv - i (minor); Imperfect (Half Cadence): I - V or IV - V (Major) and i - V or iv - V (minor)

Scores
- Rewrite a given passage into modern vocal score, string quartet score or short score (on 2 staves)

Musical Terms and Signs
- Recognize, define or supply the musical terms or signs as listed in the Advanced Rudiments Workbook

Analysis
- Analyze a short musical composition, identifying any of the above theory requirements

Score:
   60 - 69 Pass; **70 - 79** Honors; **80 - 89** First Class Honors; **90 - 100** First Class Honors with Distinction

Ultimate Music Theory: *The Way to Score Success!*

UltimateMusicTheory.com © Copyright 2013 Gloryland Publishing. All Rights Reserved.

ULTIMATE MUSIC THEORY
ADVANCED EXAM SET #2 - EXAM #1

Total Score: ___ / 100

> ♪ **UMT Tip:** Before beginning your exam, write out the Circle of Fifths. Write the order of flats and sharps. Write the Major keys on the outside of the circle and the relative minor keys on the inside of the circle.

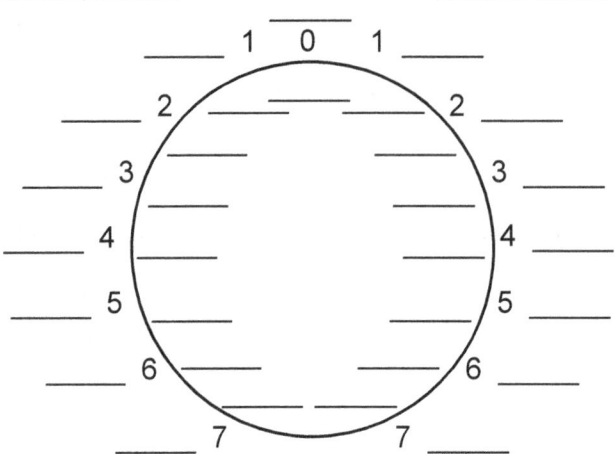

> ♪ **UMT Tip:** An inversion of a Compound interval becomes a Simple interval. A Compound interval and its inversion always equal 16.

1. a) Identify the following harmonic intervals.

b) Invert the above harmonic intervals in the same clef. Use whole notes. Name the inversions.

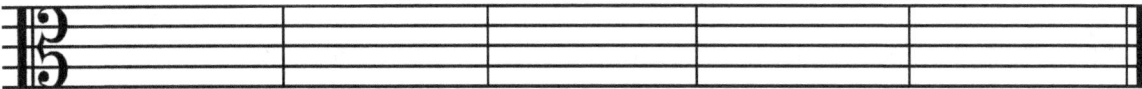

UltimateMusicTheory.com © Copyright 2013 Gloryland Publishing. All Rights Reserved.

ULTIMATE MUSIC THEORY
ADVANCED EXAM SET #2 - EXAM #1

> ♪ **UMT Tip:** To identify the position of a Dominant Seventh Chord in an inversion, add square brackets at the end of each measure. Rewrite the chord in root position. A square bracket means "I'm thinking" and does not have to be erased.

2. For each of the following Dominant Seventh chords:
   a) Name the key to which it belongs.
   b) Name the position.

Key: _____ _____ _____

Position: _____ _____ _____

Key: _____ _____ _____

Position: _____ _____ _____

> ♪ **UMT Tip:** The raised 7th (Leading Note) is a diatonic semitone below the Tonic of the harmonic minor scale.

For each of the following chords:
c) Add any necessary accidentals to form a diminished seventh chord.
d) Name the minor key to which it belongs.

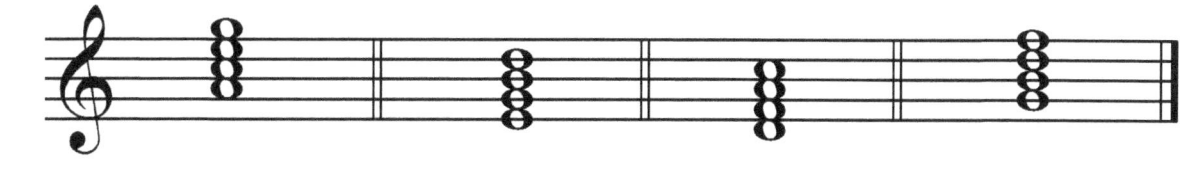

Key: _____ _____ _____ _____

UltimateMusicTheory.com © Copyright 2013 Gloryland Publishing. All Rights Reserved.

ULTIMATE MUSIC THEORY
ADVANCED EXAM SET #2 - EXAM #1

> ♪ **UMT Tip:** Draw a staff in the margin. Write the interval above or below the Tonic note of the given melody as indicated. That note names the new key.

3. a) Name the key of the following melody.
   b) Transpose the melody down an Augmented fourth, using the correct Key Signature. Name the new key.

___
10

[melody in treble clef, 3/2 time, three sharps]

Key: _____

Key: _____

> ♪ **UMT Tip:** The French Horn and English Horn are both Horns. "Horns" has 5 letters. To transpose to concert pitch, the instruments that are horns go down a Perfect 5th.

The following melody is written for French Horn in F.
c) Name the key in which it is written.
d) Transpose it to concert pitch, using the correct Key Signature. Name the new key.

[melody in treble clef, 6/8 time, one flat]

Key: _____

Key: _____

UltimateMusicTheory.com © Copyright 2013 Gloryland Publishing. All Rights Reserved.

ULTIMATE MUSIC THEORY
ADVANCED EXAM SET #2 - EXAM #1

> ♪ **UMT Tip:** When writing modes, use the "hint" sentence: I Do Play Like Mozart And Liszt. Write the letter names of the mode first, then count down to determine the Tonic note of the Major scale.

4. Write the following scales, ascending and descending. Use accidentals. Use whole notes.

   $\frac{}{10}$ a) c sharp minor melodic, from Submediant to Submediant.

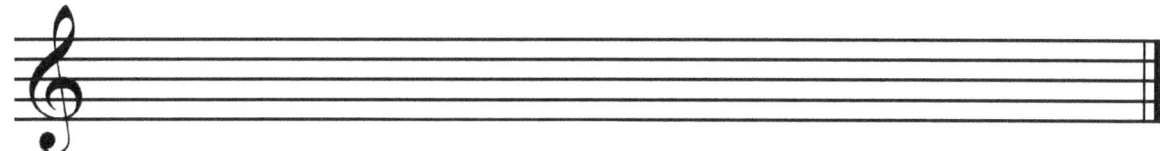

   b) The relative minor, harmonic form, of F sharp Major, from Mediant to Mediant.

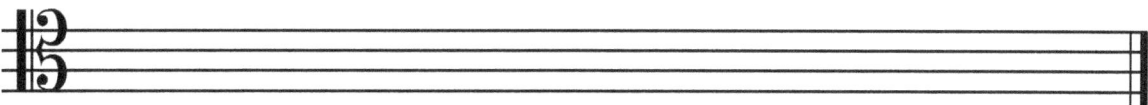

   c) Lydian mode starting on E flat. Use any standard notation.

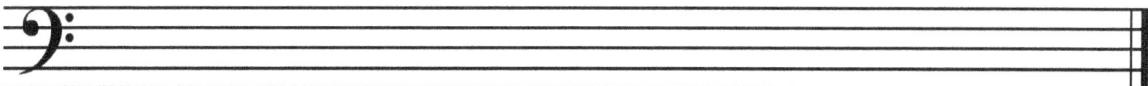

   d) Dorian mode starting on B. Use any standard notation.

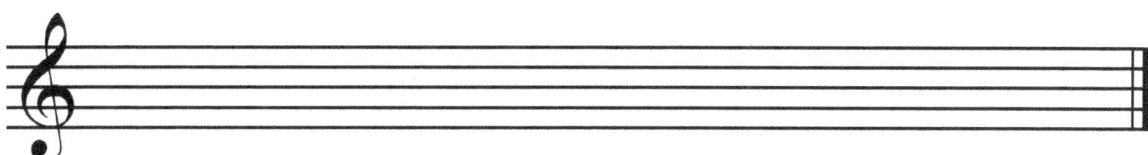

   e) Whole tone scale starting on A. Use any standard notation.

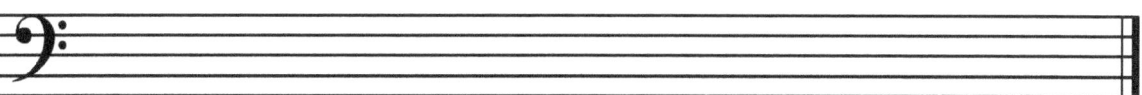

ULTIMATE MUSIC THEORY
ADVANCED EXAM SET #2 - EXAM #1

> ♪ **UMT Tip:** Always write the cadence under the given notes. Use the same note values as the given notes. If there is a Common Note (one note that is the same in both triads), write it at the same pitch when possible. If it is not possible to keep the Common Note, move all notes in the Treble Clef by 2nd or 3rd.

5. For each of the following melodic fragments:
   a) Name the key.
   b) Write a cadence in keyboard style below the notes underneath the brackets.
   c) Name the type of cadence (Perfect, Imperfect or Plagal).

$\overline{10}$

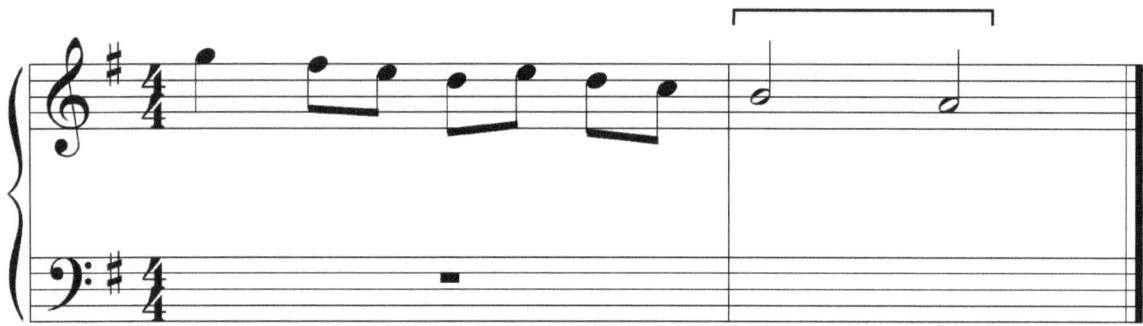

Key: _____   _____

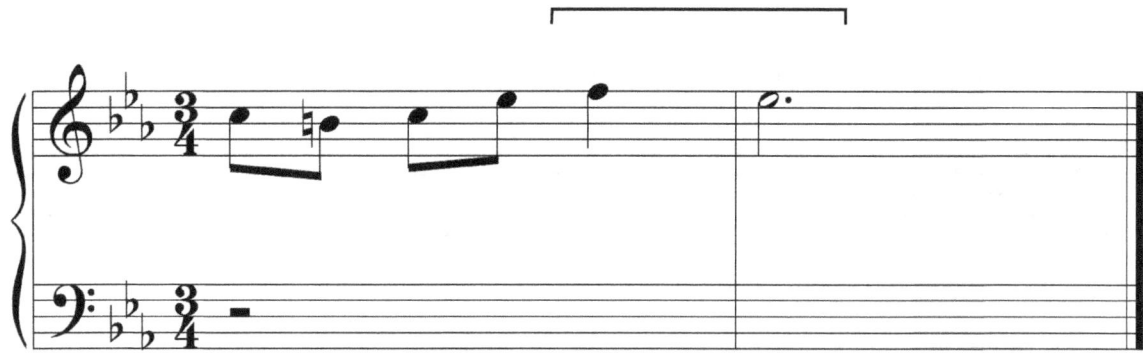

Key: _____   _____

UltimateMusicTheory.com © Copyright 2013 Gloryland Publishing. All Rights Reserved.

ULTIMATE MUSIC THEORY
ADVANCED EXAM SET #2 - EXAM #1

♪ **UMT Tip:** Use a ruler to keep all notes and bar lines vertical.

6. a) Name the key.
   b) Rewrite the following passage in Open Score for String Quartet.
   c) Name the four instruments that would play this passage. Do not use abbreviations.

Key: _____

ULTIMATE MUSIC THEORY
ADVANCED EXAM SET #2 - EXAM #1

> ♪ **UMT Tip:** Write the Basic Beat and Pulse below each measure for simple, compound or hybrid time. Cross off the Basic Beat as each beat is completed.

7. Add rests below each bracket to complete each measure.

ULTIMATE MUSIC THEORY
ADVANCED EXAM SET #2 - EXAM #1

> ♪ **UMT Tip:** A Major, minor, Augmented or diminished triad with one note doubled (usually the root note) is called a chord. For open position chords, rewrite the notes in a square bracket in close position.

8. Identify each of the following chords as a Major chord, minor chord, Augmented chord, diminished chord, Dominant Seventh chord, diminished 7th chord, quartal chord, polychord or cluster.

ULTIMATE MUSIC THEORY
ADVANCED EXAM SET #2 - EXAM #1

> ♪ **UMT Tip:** Musical terms indicate tempo, changes in tempo, pedal, articulation, dynamics and style in performance.

9. Match each musical term with its English definition. (Not all definitions will be used.)

Term **Definition**

a) above

sforzando _____   b) simple

sopra _____   c) sustained

scherzando _____   d) sonorous

semplice _____   e) very

seconda _____   f) sad

sonore _____   g) soft, subdued, under the breath

stringendo _____   h) a sudden strong accent of a single note or chord

sostenuto _____   i) second or lower part of a duet

sehr _____   j) be silent

sotto voce _____   k) playful

l) pressing, becoming faster

ULTIMATE MUSIC THEORY
ADVANCED EXAM SET #2 - EXAM #1

> ♪ **UMT Tip:** The relationship between musical passages can be imitation, inversion or sequence.

10. Analyze the following excerpt of music by answering the questions below.

Prelude in d minor

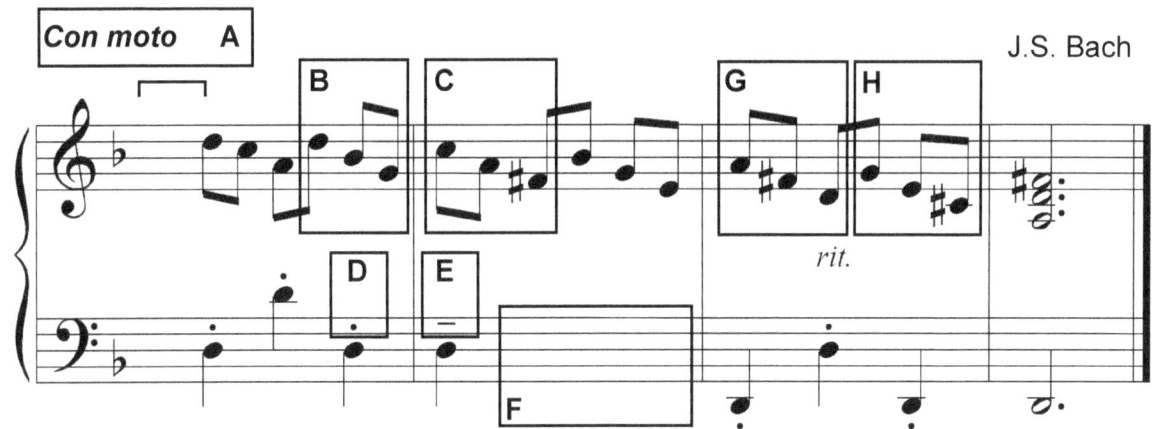

a) Explain the term at **A**. _____

b) Add the Time Signature directly on the music.

c) For the triad at **B**, name: Root: ____ Type/Quality: _____ Position: _____

d) For the triad at **C**, name: Root: ____ Type/Quality: _____ Position: _____

e) Explain the sign at **D**. _____

f) Explain the sign at **E**. _____

g) Add the missing rest(s) at **F**.

h) Give the term for the relationship between the Bass Clef at measures 1 and 3. _____

i) For the triad at **G**, name: Root: ____ Type/Quality: _____ Position: _____

j) For the triad at **H**, name: Root: ____ Type/Quality: _____ Position: _____

UltimateMusicTheory.com © Copyright 2013 Gloryland Publishing. All Rights Reserved.

ULTIMATE MUSIC THEORY
ADVANCED EXAM SET #2 - EXAM #2

Total Score: ____ / 100

1. a) Write the following intervals below each of the given notes. Use whole notes.

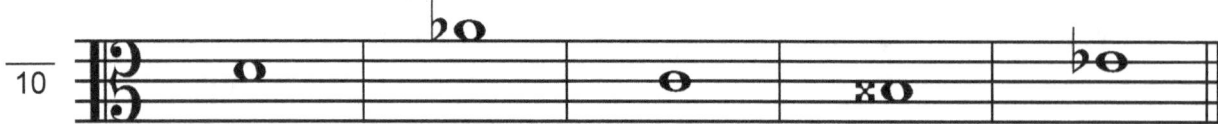

      Perfect 11   diminished 7   Major 3   Perfect 5   minor 10

b) Invert the above intervals in the Treble Clef. Name the inversions.

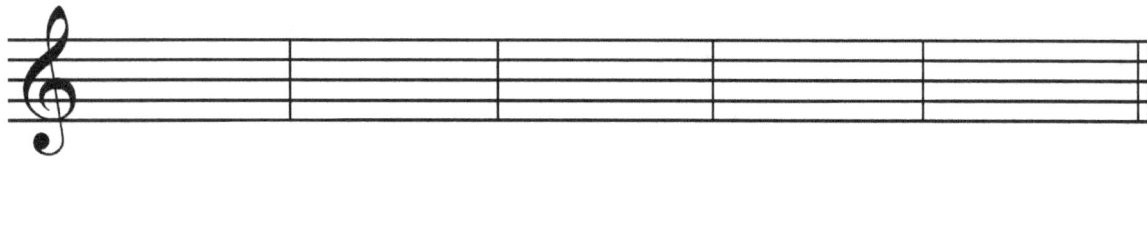

   _____   _____   _____   _____   _____

c) Write the following intervals above each of the given notes. Use whole notes.

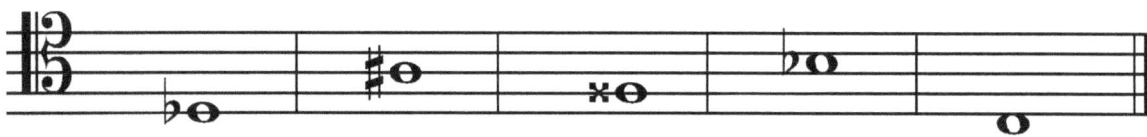

      Major 14   minor 6   Perfect 8   Augmented 5   diminished 12

d) Invert the above intervals in the Bass Clef. Name the inversions.

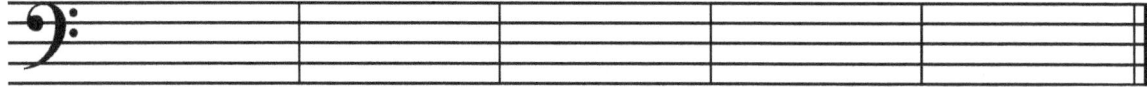

   _____   _____   _____   _____   _____

UltimateMusicTheory.com © Copyright 2013 Gloryland Publishing. All Rights Reserved.

ULTIMATE MUSIC THEORY
ADVANCED EXAM SET #2 - EXAM #2

2. Write the following chords in the Treble Clef. Use accidentals. Use whole notes.

   a) The Dominant 7th chord of G Major in third inversion.

   b) The diminished 7th chord of c sharp minor harmonic in root position.

   c) The Dominant 7th chord of B flat Major in second inversion.

   d) The diminished 7th chord of e flat minor harmonic in root position.

   e) The Dominant 7th chord of f sharp minor harmonic in first inversion.

Write the following chords in the Bass Clef. Use a Key Signature. Use whole notes.

   f) The Dominant 7th chord of D Major in first inversion.

   g) The diminished 7th chord of e minor harmonic in root position.

   h) The Dominant 7th chord of f minor harmonic in second inversion.

   i) The diminished 7th chord of d minor harmonic in root position.

   j) The Dominant 7th chord of G Major in third inversion.

ULTIMATE MUSIC THEORY
ADVANCED EXAM SET #2 - EXAM #2

3. a) Name the key of the following melody.
   b) Rewrite the melody at the same pitch in the Treble Clef.

Key: _____

The following melody is written for Clarinet in B flat.
c) Name the key in which it is written.
d) Transpose it to concert pitch, using the correct Key Signature. Name the new key.

Key: _____

Key: _____

ULTIMATE MUSIC THEORY
ADVANCED EXAM SET #2 - EXAM #2

4. For each of the following Major, minor harmonic or minor melodic scales:
   a) Identify the Major or minor key.
   b) Identify the Technical Degree Name of the starting note. Do not use abbreviations.

i) Key: _____ Technical Degree: _____

ii) Key: _____ Technical Degree: _____

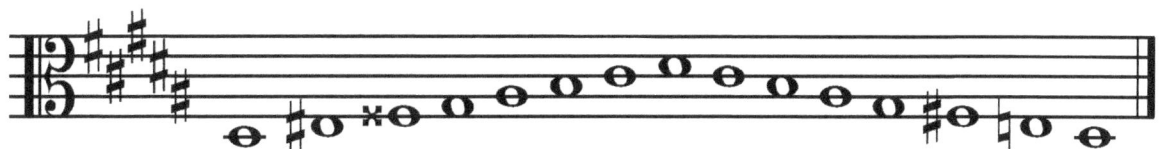

iii) Key: _____ Technical Degree: _____

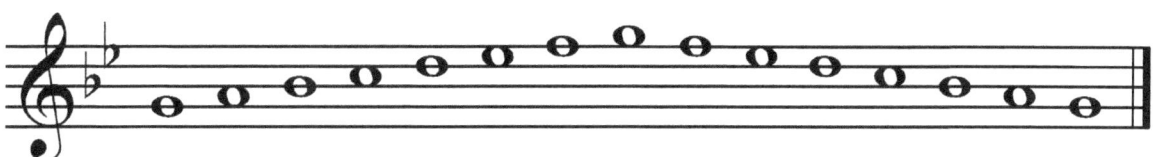

iv) Key: _____ Technical Degree: _____

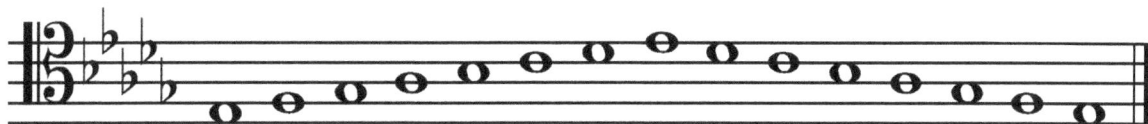

v) Key: _____ Technical Degree: _____

ULTIMATE MUSIC THEORY
ADVANCED EXAM SET #2 - EXAM #2

5. For each of the following melodic fragments:
   a) Name the key.
   b) Write the Roman Numerals below the Chords underneath the bracket.
   c) Name the type of cadence (Perfect, Imperfect or Plagal).

$\overline{10}$

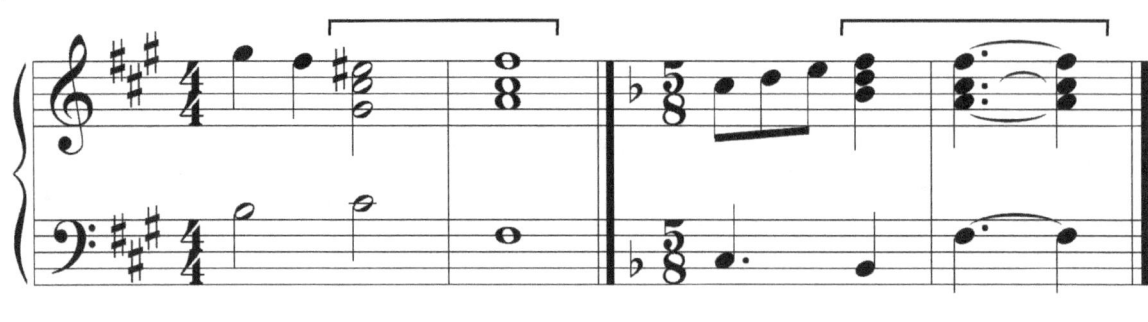

a) _____ b) _____ _____   a) _____ b) _____ _____

c) _____   c) _____

a) _____ b) _____ _____   a) _____ b) _____ _____

c) _____   c) _____

a) _____   b) _____ _____

c) _____

UltimateMusicTheory.com © Copyright 2013 Gloryland Publishing. All Rights Reserved.

ULTIMATE MUSIC THEORY
ADVANCED EXAM SET #2 - EXAM #2

6. Rewrite the following passage in Short Score (using two staves).

For a Thousand Tongues to Sing

Moderato

T. Haweis

ULTIMATE MUSIC THEORY
ADVANCED EXAM SET #2 - EXAM #2

7. Add rests below each bracket to complete each measure.

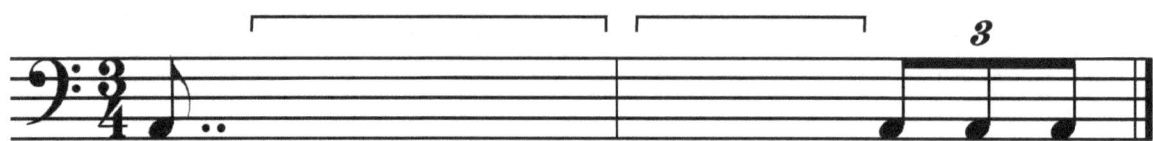

ULTIMATE MUSIC THEORY
ADVANCED EXAM SET #2 - EXAM #2

8. For each of the following triads, name:
   a) the root.
   b) the quality/type (Maj, min, Aug or dim).
   c) the position (root pos, 1st inv or 2nd inv).

   /10

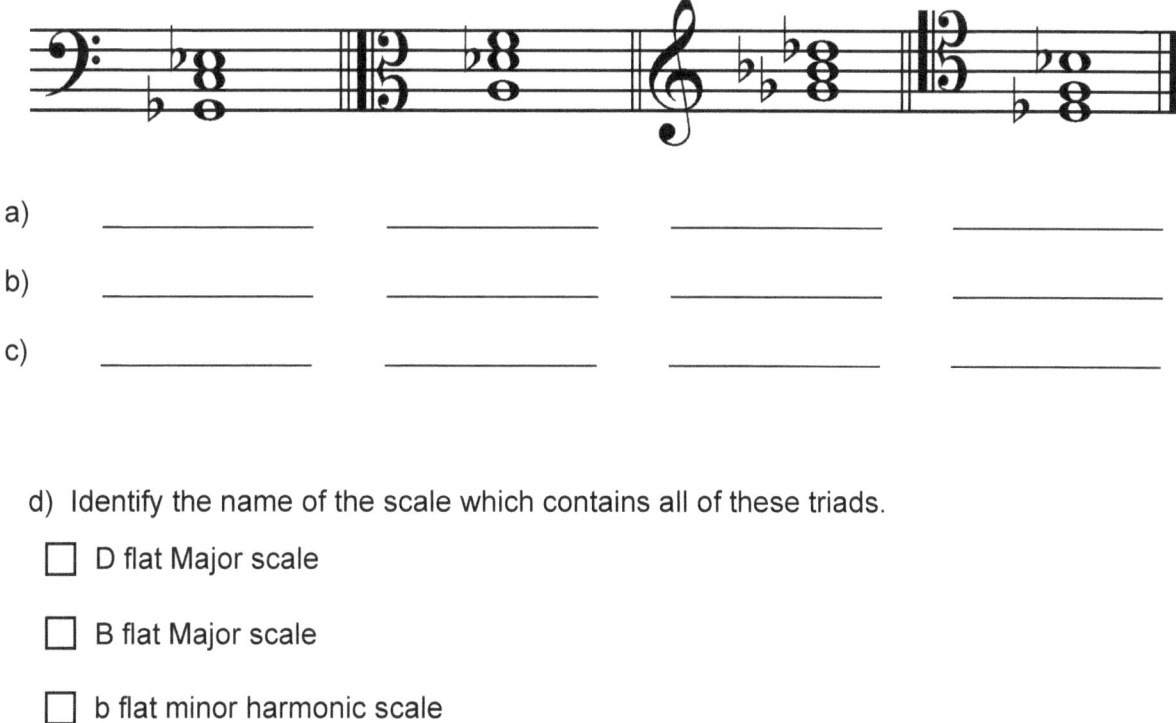

a) _____   _____   _____   _____

b) _____   _____   _____   _____

c) _____   _____   _____   _____

d) Identify the name of the scale which contains all of these triads.

☐ D flat Major scale

☐ B flat Major scale

☐ b flat minor harmonic scale

☐ d flat minor harmonic scale

e) Name each of the following chords as Dominant seventh chord, diminished seventh chord, quartal chord, polychord or cluster chord.

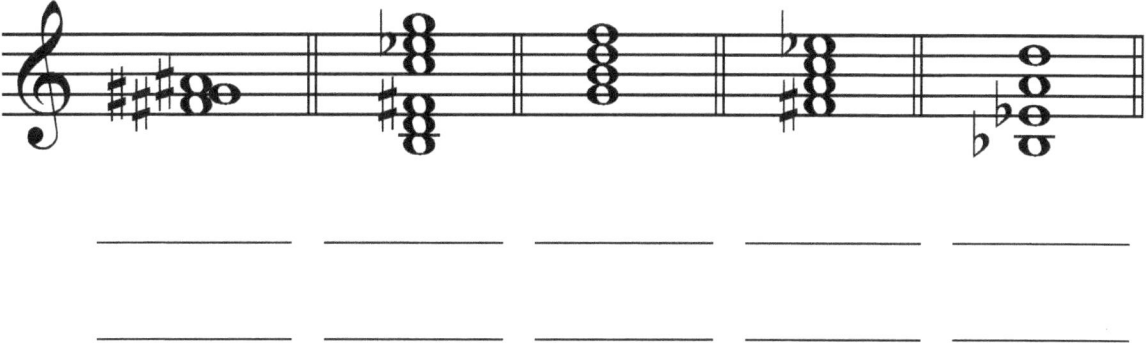

_____   _____   _____   _____   _____

_____   _____   _____   _____   _____

ULTIMATE MUSIC THEORY
ADVANCED EXAM SET #2 - EXAM #2

9. Give the English definition for TEN of the following musical terms.

Term	Definition
cédez	_____
bewegt	_____
vite	_____
schnell	_____
mit Ausdruck	_____
modéré	_____
lentement	_____
sehr	_____
langsam	_____
léger	_____
mässig	_____
mouvement	_____

(10)

ULTIMATE MUSIC THEORY
ADVANCED EXAM SET #2 - EXAM #2

10. Analyze the following musical excerpt by answering the questions below.

Bagatelle

Ludwig van Beethoven

Allegretto

a) Name the key of this piece. _____

b) Explain the tempo of this piece. _____

c) Add the Time Signature directly on the music.

d) Identify the type of chord at **A**. _____

e) For the triad at **B**, name: Root: ____ Type/Quality: _____ Position: _____

f) Explain the sign at **C**. _____

g) For the triad at **D**, name: Root: ____ Type/Quality: _____ Position: _____

h) Name the intervals at the letters: **E** _____   **F** _____

i) How many slurs are in this excerpt? _____

j) How many ties are in this excerpt? _____

UltimateMusicTheory.com © Copyright 2013 Gloryland Publishing. All Rights Reserved.

ULTIMATE MUSIC THEORY
ADVANCED EXAM SET #2 - EXAM #3

Total Score: ___ / 100

1. a) Name the following intervals.

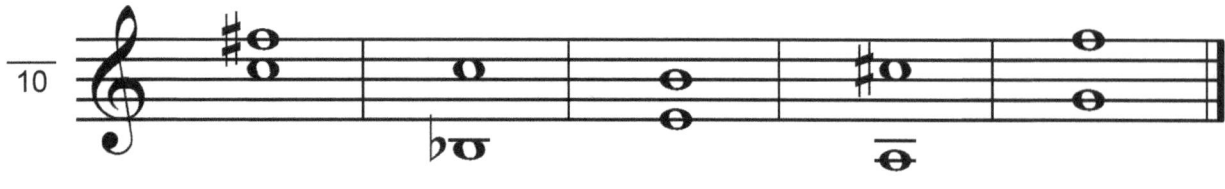

___ ___ ___ ___ ___

b) Change the upper note of each interval enharmonically. Rename the intervals.

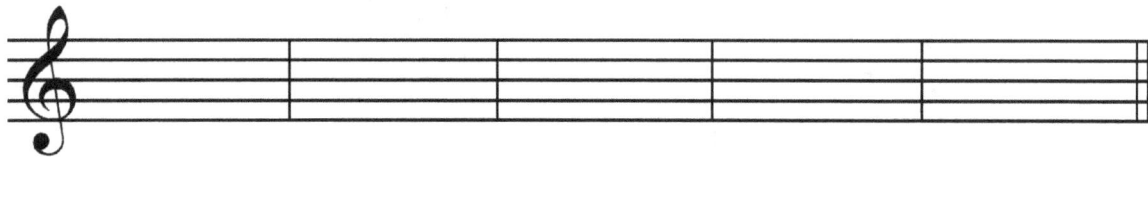

___ ___ ___ ___ ___

c) Name the following intervals.

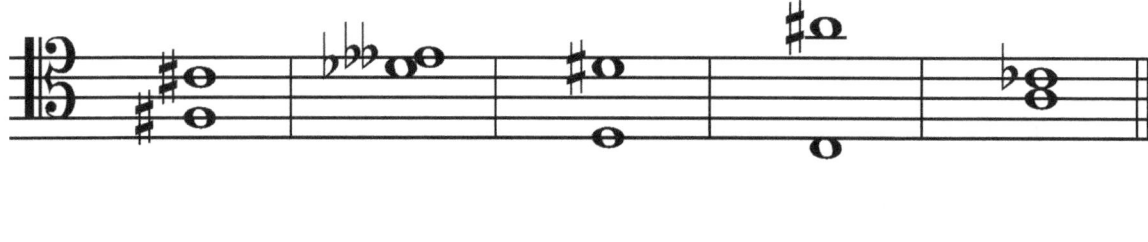

___ ___ ___ ___ ___

d) Invert the above intervals in the Bass Clef. Name the inversions.

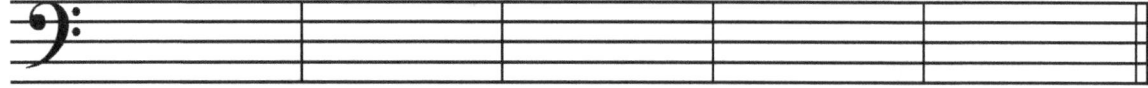

___ ___ ___ ___ ___

ULTIMATE MUSIC THEORY
ADVANCED EXAM SET #2 - EXAM #3

2. For each of the following Dominant Seventh chords, name:
   a) the key.
   b) the position.

a) _____ _____ _____ _____ _____

b) _____ _____ _____ _____ _____

For each of the following diminished seventh chords, name:
c) the key.
d) the position.

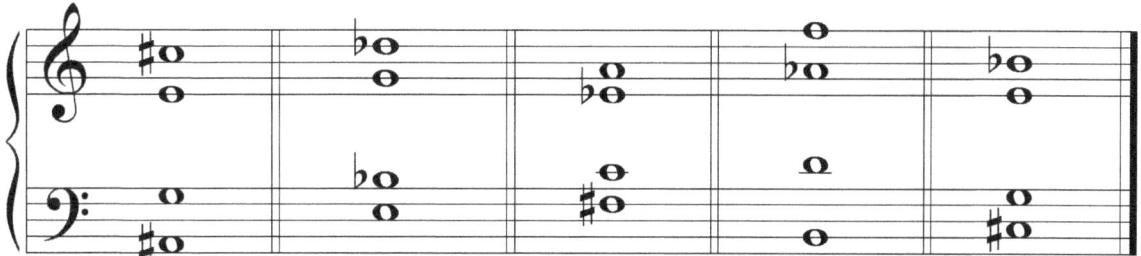

c) _____ _____ _____ _____ _____

d) _____ _____ _____ _____ _____

ULTIMATE MUSIC THEORY
ADVANCED EXAM SET #2 - EXAM #3

3. a) Name the key of the following melody.
   b) Rewrite the melody at the same pitch in the Bass Clef.

Key: _____

The following melody is written for English Horn in F.
c) Name the key in which it is written.
d) Transpose it to concert pitch, using the correct Key Signature. Name the new key.

Key: _____

Key: _____

ULTIMATE MUSIC THEORY
ADVANCED EXAM SET #2 - EXAM #3

4. Add the clef, Key Signature and any necessary accidentals to form the following scales.

___
10

a) b minor harmonic scale from Submediant to Submediant.

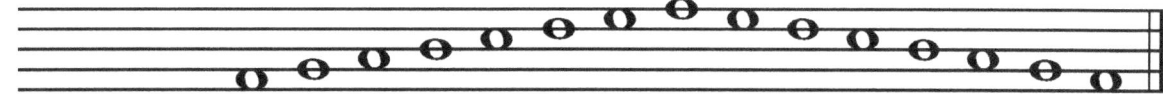

b) b flat minor melodic scale from Supertonic to Supertonic.

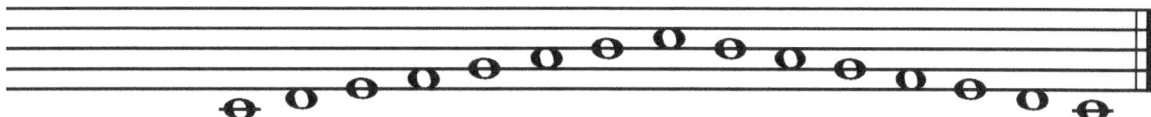

c) B Major scale from Subdominant to Subdominant.

d) Name the following modes as Dorian, Phrygian, Lydian, Moxolydian or Aeolian.

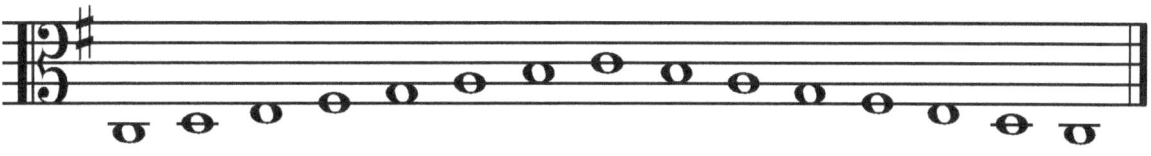

_____

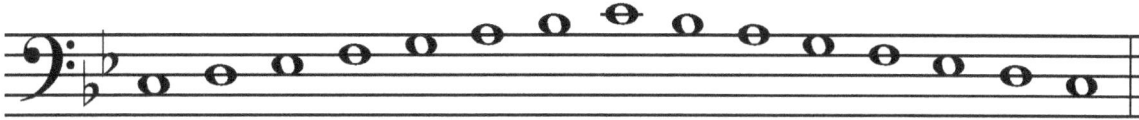

_____

ULTIMATE MUSIC THEORY
ADVANCED EXAM SET #2 - EXAM #3

5. For each of the following melodic fragments:
   a) Name the key.
   b) Write a cadence in Keyboard Style below the bracketed notes.
   c) Name the type of cadence (Perfect, Imperfect or Plagal).

$\overline{10}$

Key: _____   _____

Key: _____   _____

ULTIMATE MUSIC THEORY
ADVANCED EXAM SET #2 - EXAM #3

6. Rewrite the following passage in Short Score (using two staves).

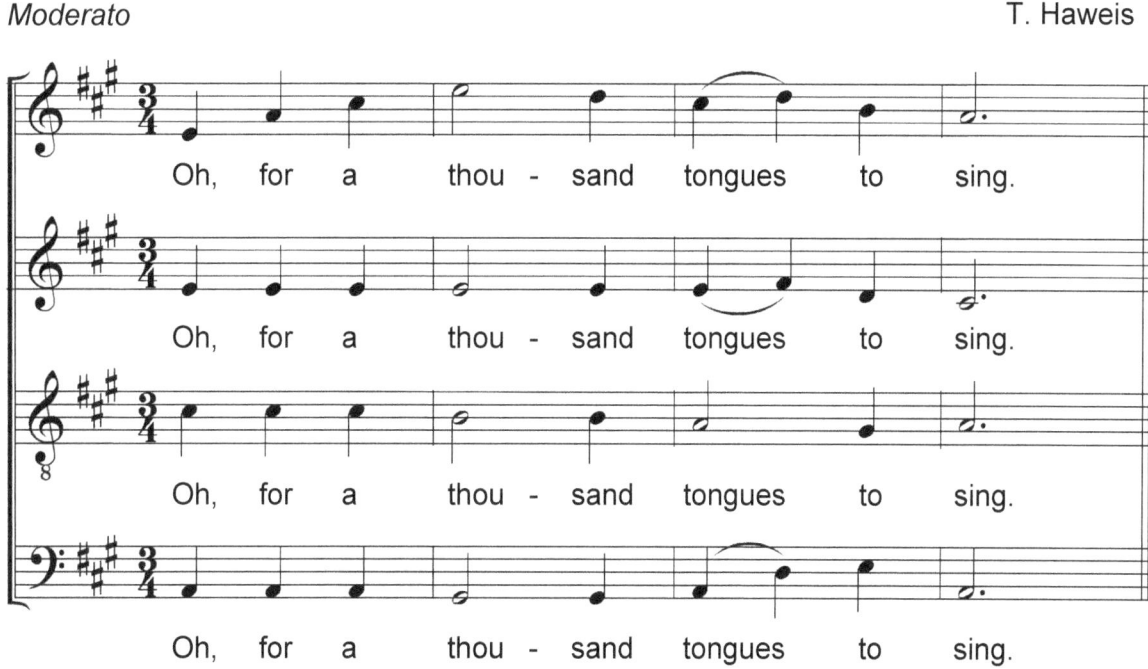

For a Thousand Tongues to Sing

Moderato

T. Haweis

ULTIMATE MUSIC THEORY
ADVANCED EXAM SET #2 - EXAM #3

7. a) Add rests below each bracket to complete each measure.

b) Add the correct Time Signature at the beginning of each of the following excerpts.

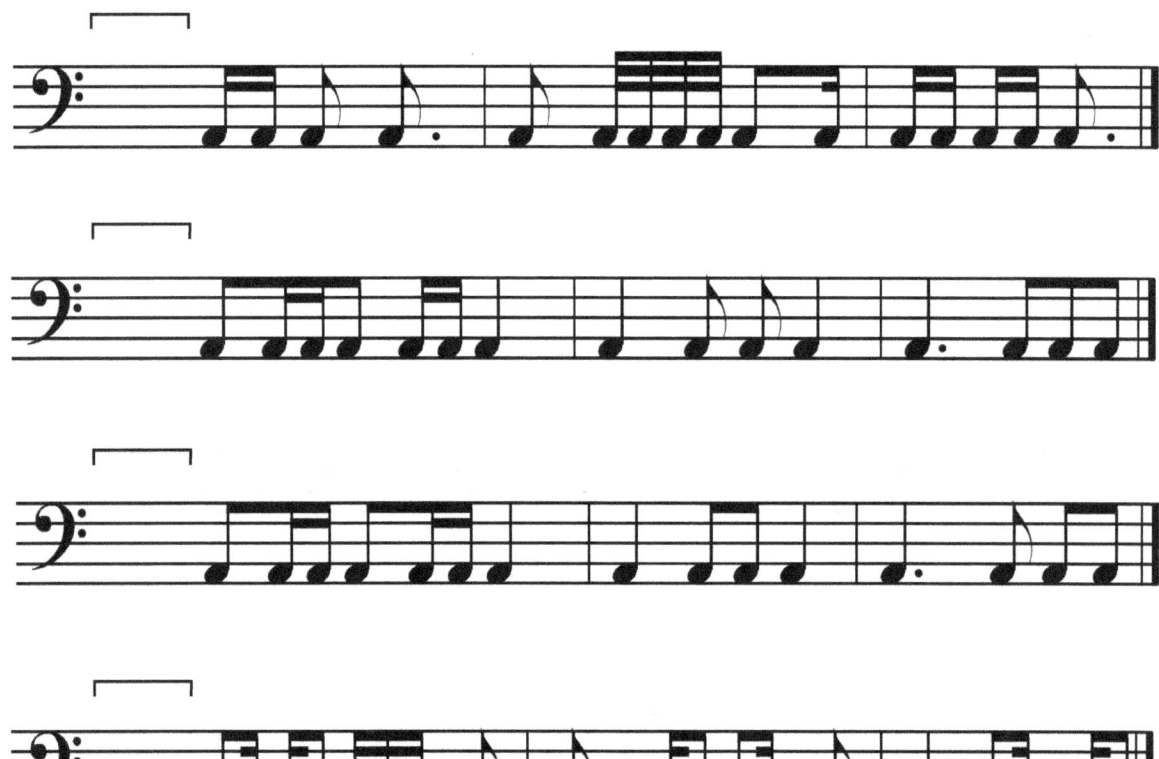

ULTIMATE MUSIC THEORY
ADVANCED EXAM SET #2 - EXAM #3

8. For each of the following triads, name:
   a) the root.
   b) the quality/type (Major, minor, Augmented or diminished).

___
10

Tonic triad of G flat Major	Root: _____	Quality/Type: _____
Submediant triad of e flat minor harmonic	Root: _____	Quality/Type: _____
Leading Note triad of b minor harmonic	Root: _____	Quality/Type: _____
Mediant triad of E Major	Root: _____	Quality/Type: _____
Dominant triad of C sharp Major	Root: _____	Quality/Type: _____
Submediant triad of E flat Major	Root: _____	Quality/Type: _____
Leading Note triad of B Major	Root: _____	Quality/Type: _____
Dominant triad of c sharp minor harmonic	Root: _____	Quality/Type: _____
Supertonic triad of d minor harmonic	Root: _____	Quality/Type: _____
Subdominant triad of b flat minor harmonic	Root: _____	Quality/Type: _____

ULTIMATE MUSIC THEORY
ADVANCED EXAM SET #2 - EXAM #3

9. Match each musical term or sign with its English definition. (Not all definitions will be used.)

Term		Definition
		a) loud, then suddenly soft
sf	_____	b) broadening, becoming slower
v.s.	_____	c) one octave higher
allarg.	_____	d) two octaves higher
ad lib.	_____	e) turn the page quickly
𝒫𝑒𝒹.	_____	f) left hand
fp	_____	g) right hand
𝄋	_____	h) a sudden strong accent of a single note or chord
M.D.	_____	i) from the sign
15ma	_____	j) at the liberty of the performer
M.S.	_____	k) pedal marking
		l) in the manner of

ULTIMATE MUSIC THEORY
ADVANCED EXAM SET #2 - EXAM #3

10. Analyze the following musical excerpt by answering the questions below.

Contradance
Ludwig van Beethoven

a) Name the key of this piece. _____

b) Add the Time Signature directly on the music.

c) Identify the term at **A**. _____

d) For the triad at **B**, name: Root: _____ Type/Quality: _____ Position: _____

e) Explain the sign at **C**. _____

f) Explain the sign at **D**. _____

g) Explain the sign at **E**. _____

h) For the triad at **F**, name: Root: _____ Type/Quality: _____ Position: _____

i) Explain the sign at **G**. _____

j) How many slurs are in this excerpt? _____

UltimateMusicTheory.com © Copyright 2013 Gloryland Publishing. All Rights Reserved.

ULTIMATE MUSIC THEORY
ADVANCED EXAM SET #2 - EXAM #4

Total Score: ___ / 100

1. a) Name the following intervals.

___ ___ ___ ___ ___

b) Invert the intervals in the Treble Clef. Use whole notes. Name the inversions.

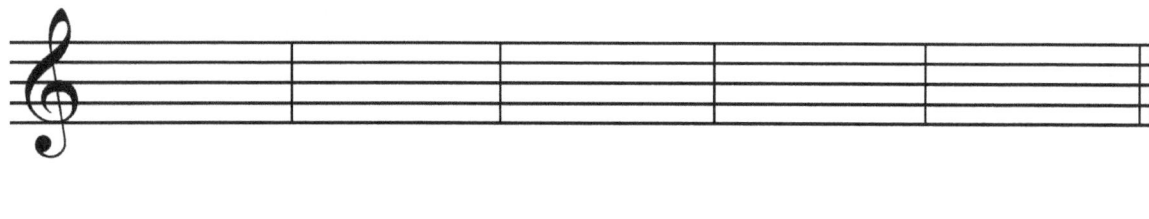

___ ___ ___ ___ ___

c) Name the following intervals.

___ ___ ___ ___ ___

d) Change the lower note of each interval enharmonically. Rename the intervals.

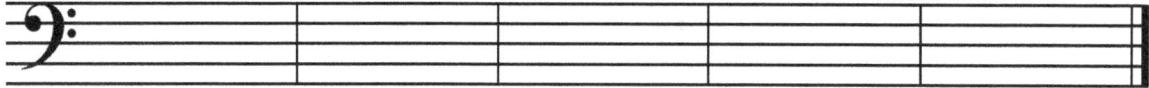

___ ___ ___ ___ ___

UltimateMusicTheory.com © Copyright 2013 Gloryland Publishing. All Rights Reserved.

ULTIMATE MUSIC THEORY
ADVANCED EXAM SET #2 - EXAM #4

2. For each of the following Dominant Seventh chords, name:
   a) the Major key.
   b) the minor key.
   c) the position.

___
10

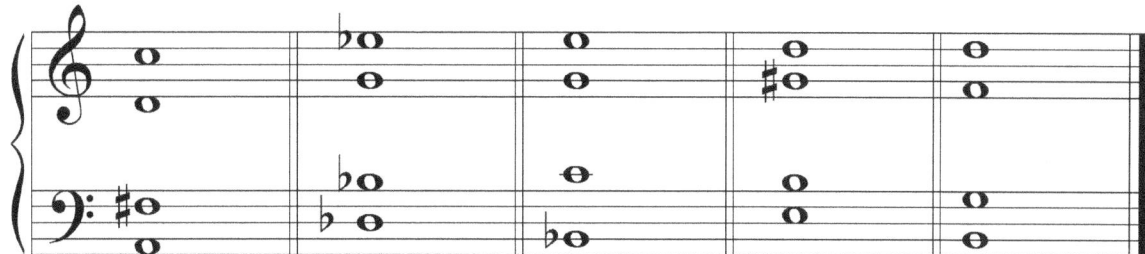

a) _____ _____ _____ _____ _____

b) _____ _____ _____ _____ _____

c) _____ _____ _____ _____ _____

For each of the following diminished seventh chords, name:
d) the minor key.

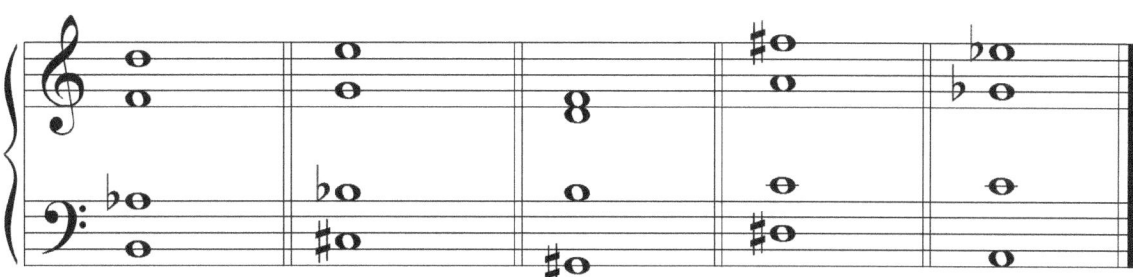

d) _____ _____ _____ _____ _____

3. The following melody is written using accidentals.
   a) Name the key.
   b) Rewrite the melody using a Key Signature.

Key: _____

The following melody is written for French Horn in F.
c) Name the key in which it is written.
d) Transpose it to concert pitch, using the correct Key Signature. Name the new key.

Key: _____

Key: _____

ULTIMATE MUSIC THEORY
ADVANCED EXAM SET #2 - EXAM #4

4. Write the following scales and modes. Use accidentals. Use whole notes.

a) Relative Major of b flat minor in the Alto Clef.

___
10

b) Tonic minor, melodic form, of C sharp Major in the Bass Clef.

c) Enharmonic Tonic minor, harmonic form, of g sharp minor in the Tenor Clef.

d) Lydian mode starting on C in the Treble Clef.

e) Mixolydian mode starting on F in the Bass Clef.

ULTIMATE MUSIC THEORY
ADVANCED EXAM SET #2 - EXAM #4

5. For each of the following melodic fragments:
   a) Name the key.
   b) Write a cadence in Keyboard Style below the bracketed notes.
   c) Name the type of cadence (Perfect, Imperfect or Plagal).

/10

Key: _____   _____

Key: _____   _____

ULTIMATE MUSIC THEORY
ADVANCED EXAM SET #2 - EXAM #4

6. For each of the following chords:
   a) Name the chord type as: triad, Dominant seventh chord, diminished seventh chord, cluster or quartal chord.
   b) Rewrite the chord in the specified type of open score.
   c) Name each voice/instrument in the open score. Do not use abbreviations.

Modern Vocal Score

Chord Type:

_____

Open Score for String Quartet

Chord Type:

_____

ULTIMATE MUSIC THEORY
ADVANCED EXAM SET #2 - EXAM #4

7. a) Add rests below each bracket to complete each measure.

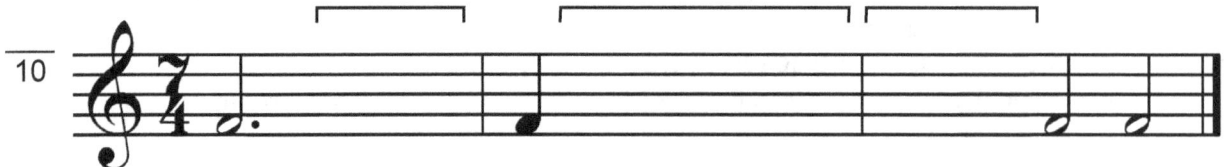

b) Add the correct Time Signature at the beginning of each of the following excerpts.

ULTIMATE MUSIC THEORY
ADVANCED EXAM SET #2 - EXAM #4

8. For each of the following triads, name:
   a) the root.
   b) the quality/type (Major, minor, Augmented or diminished).
   c) the position (root pos, 1st inv or 2nd inv).

a) _____   _____   _____   _____

b) _____   _____   _____   _____

c) _____   _____   _____   _____

d) Identify the name of the scale which contains all of these triads.

☐ B Major scale

☐ E Major scale

☐ g sharp minor harmonic scale

☐ c sharp minor harmonic scale

e) Name each of the following chords as Dominant seventh chord, diminished seventh chord, quartal chord, polychord or cluster chord.

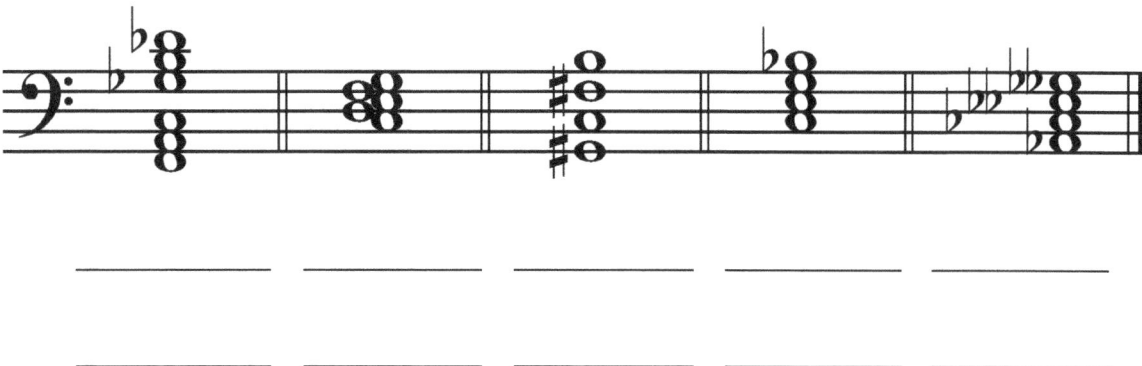

_____   _____   _____   _____   _____

ULTIMATE MUSIC THEORY
ADVANCED EXAM SET #2 - EXAM #4

9. Match each musical term with its English definition. (Not all definitions will be used.)

$\overline{10}$

Term		Definition
		a) dying, fading away
accelerando	_____	b) becoming slower and softer
attacca	_____	c) lively
calando	_____	d) weighty, with emphasis
con fuoco	_____	e) with fire
vivo	_____	f) almost, as if
volta	_____	g) proceed without a break
morendo	_____	h) two octaves higher
mesto	_____	i) first; the upper part of a duet
quasi	_____	j) becoming quicker
quindicesima alta	_____	k) time
		l) sad, mournful

ULTIMATE MUSIC THEORY
ADVANCED EXAM SET #2 - EXAM #4

10. Analyze the following piece of music by answering the questions below.

Merry-Go-Round

S. McKibbon

Con moto

a) Name the key of this piece. _____

b) Explain the tempo of this piece. _____

c) Add the Time Signature directly on the music.

d) Give the term for the relationship between the notes at the letters **A** and **B**. _____

e) Give the technical degree for the note at the letter **C**. _____

f) Name the interval at the letter **D**. _____

g) For the triad at **E**, name: Root: ____ Type/Quality: _____ Position: _____

h) Explain the sign at the letter **F**. _____

i) Identify the cadence at the letter **G**. _____

j) Locate and circle a Tritone. Name the interval. _____

Workbooks, Exams, Answers, Online Courses, App & More!

A Proven Step-by-Step System to Learn Theory Faster - from Beginner to Advanced.

Innovative techniques designed to develop a complete understanding of music theory, to enhance sight reading, ear training, creativity, composition and musical expression.

All UMT Series have matching Answer Books!

The UMT Rudiments Series - Beginner A, Beginner B, Beginner C, Prep 1, Prep 2, Basic, Intermediate, Advanced & Complete (All-In-One)

♪ 12 Lessons, Review Tests, and a Final Exam to develop confidence
♪ Music Theory Guide & Chart for fast and easy reference of theory concepts
♪ 80 Flashcards for fun drills to dramatically increase retention & comprehension

Rudiments Exam Series - Preparatory, Basic, Intermediate & Advanced

♪ 8 Exams plus UMT Tips on How to Score 100% on Theory Exams

Each Rudiments Workbook correlates to a Supplemental Workbook.

The UMT Supplemental Series - Prep Level, Level 1, Level 2, Level 3, Level 4, Level 5, Level 6, Level 7, Level 8 & Complete (All-In-One) Level

♪ Form & Analysis and Music History - Composers, Eras & Musical Styles
♪ Melody Writing using ICE - Imagine, Compose & Explore
♪ 12 Lessons, Review Tests, Final Exam and 80 Flashcards for quick study

Supplemental Exam Series - Level 5, Level 6, Level 7 & Level 8

♪ 8 Exams to successfully prepare for nationally recognized Theory Exams

UMT Online Courses, Music Theory App & More

♪ UMT Certification Course, Teachers Membership & Elite Educator Program
♪ Ultimate Music Theory App correlates to the Rudiments Workbooks
♪ Free Resources - Teachers Guide, Music Theory Blogs, videos & downloads

Go To: **UltimateMusicTheory.com**

www.ingramcontent.com/pod-product-compliance
Lightning Source LLC
Chambersburg PA
CBHW081735100526
44591CB00016B/2619